MW00960428

HALLOWEL͟͟͟ ͟͟͟ ͟͟͟ STORIES FOR KIDS AGED 6-10.

Spooky Collection of Tales and Adventures for young readers for a Fun-Filled Halloween.

M. Samantha

Copyright © 2024 by M. Samantha

All rights reserved. No part of this publication may be reproduced, distributed, or transmitted in any form or by any means, including photocopying, recording, or other electronic or mechanical methods, without the prior written permission of the publisher, except in the case of brief quotations embodied in critical reviews and certain other noncommercial uses permitted by copyright law.

TABLE OF CONTENT

The Haunted Candy Quest

It was Halloween night, and Tommy, Lily, and Ben were on a mission to collect as much candy as possible. They'd planned their route for weeks, targeting the houses that gave out the best treats. They laughed and raced from house to house, their bags growing heavier with each stop.

As they reached the last house on their list, an old, creaky mansion at the end of the street, they hesitated. The house was dark and covered in cobwebs, with a rusted gate that groaned when pushed open. But their desire for more candy outweighed their fear.

An old woman with wild gray hair and a crooked smile opened the door. She looked at them with piercing eyes and handed each of them a small piece of candy wrapped in silver foil.

"Eat this only when you're ready for an adventure," she said, her voice a raspy whisper.

The kids exchanged curious glances but thanked her and hurried away, eager to get back to the brightly lit streets. They didn't think much about the strange encounter as they continued trick-or-treating.

Back at Tommy's house, the three friends dumped their bags of candy on the floor and began sorting through their loot. Among the piles of chocolate bars, gummies, and lollipops, they each found the silver-wrapped candy from the old woman's house.

"What do you think she meant by 'ready for an adventure'?" Lily asked.

"Maybe it's just a trick to make us think it's special," Ben suggested.

"Well, there's only one way to find out," Tommy said, unwrapping his candy. The others followed his lead.

As soon as they popped the candy into their mouths, the room spun around them. Colors blurred, and a strange, cold breeze filled the air. When the spinning stopped, they found themselves no longer in Tommy's living room but in a dark, misty forest.

"What just happened?" Ben gasped, looking around in shock.

"I think... we're in the adventure," Lily whispered, her eyes wide with fear.

The forest was eerily quiet, except for the occasional rustle of leaves. Shadows danced among the trees, and strange, glowing eyes watched them from the darkness.

"Okay, this is creepy," Tommy said, trying to keep his voice steady. "We need to figure out how to get back home."

As they began to walk, the path ahead of them split into three, each leading in a different direction. At the crossroads stood a ghostly figure, a pale, translucent boy about their age.

"Hello," the ghost said in a sad voice. "I'm Henry. I've been stuck here for years, trying to return the candy I stole to its rightful owners."

"The candy?" Lily asked, holding up the silver-wrapped candy, now back in her hand despite having eaten it.

"Yes," Henry replied. "The candy you have belongs to the spirits of this forest. They gave it to the old woman as a test. Only those who are brave enough to return it can leave."

"So we have to give it back?" Tommy asked.

"Yes," said Henry, "but beware, the forest is full of tricks and traps. Follow the right path, and you'll find the spirits. Choose the wrong one, and you'll be lost forever."

The kids looked at the three paths, each one darker and more foreboding than the last. They had to choose wisely.

"I think we should take the middle path," Lily suggested. "It looks the least dangerous."

Ben nodded in agreement, and Tommy shrugged. "Middle path it is."

As they walked down the middle path, the forest grew darker, and the air grew colder. Suddenly, the ground beneath them gave way, and they slid down a steep slope into a cavernous tunnel.

They landed in a large underground chamber filled with glowing mushrooms and strange, echoing sounds. In the center of the room stood a tall, shadowy figure, its face hidden beneath a hood.

"Who dares enter my domain?" the figure boomed.

"We're here to return the candy," Tommy said, his voice shaking. "We didn't mean to take it."

The figure reached out a bony hand, and Tommy quickly placed the candy in its palm. The shadowy figure inspected it closely, then nodded.

"You have done well," the figure said. "But your journey is not yet over. You must face one final challenge."

The shadowy figure waved its hand, and the chamber around them transformed into a maze of mirrors. Each reflection showed different versions of the kids—some scared, some brave, some completely unlike themselves.

"Find the true reflection, and you will be free," the figure's voice echoed through the maze.

The kids wandered through the maze, each reflection more confusing than the last. They had to rely on their instincts, their bond, and their courage.

Finally, they came upon a mirror that showed them as they truly were—nervous but determined, scared but ready to face whatever came next.

"This is it," Lily said, touching the mirror.

The mirror rippled like water, and suddenly they were back in Tommy's living room, the candy wrappers lying empty on the floor.

The three friends looked around, relieved to be back home. They couldn't believe the adventure they had just experienced.

"Was it all real?" Ben asked, still holding the empty candy wrapper.

"I think so," Tommy replied. "And I think we did something important."

Lily nodded. "We helped the ghost boy and returned the candy."

As they sat down to enjoy the rest of their Halloween candy, they couldn't help but feel a little different—braver, stronger, and closer than ever before. And as they looked out the window, they thought they saw a faint figure waving goodbye from the shadows of the trees.

The Pumpkin Patch Mystery

Every year, the town of Willow Creek held a grand pumpkin festival on Halloween. It was the highlight of the season, with families coming from miles around to pick the biggest, brightest pumpkins, carve them into jack-o'-lanterns, and enjoy the festivities. But this year, something strange was happening.

As Mia, Jake, and Ella walked through the pumpkin patch, they noticed that many of the pumpkins were missing. The once full and vibrant patch now looked oddly bare, with empty spaces where pumpkins should have been.

"Where are all the pumpkins?" Jake asked, scratching his head.

"I don't know," Mia replied, her brow furrowed in concern. "But something's definitely wrong. They were all here yesterday."

Ella, who was always the curious one, knelt down to examine the ground where a pumpkin had once been. "Look," she said, pointing at the dirt. "There are strange tracks here."

The tracks were long and winding, leading out of the pumpkin patch and into the dense woods at the edge of the farm.

"What do you think made these?" Mia asked.

"Whatever it was, it took the pumpkins," Jake said, looking around nervously. "But why would anyone steal pumpkins?"

"There's only one way to find out," Ella said, standing up with a determined look on her face. "We need to follow the tracks and solve this mystery."

Mia and Jake exchanged glances. They weren't surc what they'd find in the woods, but their curiosity got the best of them. Together, they agreed to follow the tracks and uncover the truth behind the disappearing pumpkins.

The three friends carefully made their way through the woods, following the strange tracks as they go deeper into the forest. The trees grew taller and closer together, blocking out most of the sunlight, casting eerie shadows along the path.

"This is starting to feel like a bad idea," Jake muttered, looking around warily.

"Don't be scared," Mia reassured him, though she wasn't entirely sure herself. "We're just investigating. We'll figure this out and get back in time for the festival."

As they continued walking, the tracks became more distinct, leading them to a clearing deep in the forest. In the middle of the clearing, they saw something that made them all gasp in surprise.

There, standing among the trees, was a giant pumpkin-headed creature. It had a large, glowing jack-o'-lantern for a head and a body made of twisted vines and leaves. Its eyes glowed with an eerie orange light as it looked down at them, seemingly sad rather than menacing.

"Whoa!" Jake exclaimed, taking a step back. "What is that thing?"

"I think it's a pumpkin golem," Ella whispered, her eyes wide with fascination. "My grandma told me stories about creatures like this. They're protectors of the harvest, but they're supposed to be good. Why would it be taking the pumpkins?"

The pumpkin-headed creature looked at them with a sorrowful expression and then spoke in a deep, rumbling voice. "I am the Guardian of the Patch," it said. "I have taken the pumpkins to protect them, for I am incomplete."

Mia, Jake, and Ella were startled but curious. "Incomplete?" Mia asked. "What do you mean?"

The Guardian pointed to its pumpkin head. "This is not my true head," it explained. "Many years ago, my real head was stolen by a wicked sorcerer. Without it, I cannot protect the harvest properly. I have tried to replace it with other pumpkins, but they are not the same. I feared the pumpkins would be taken as well, so I hid them here."

Ella's heart softened as she listened to the Guardian's tale. "That's why the pumpkins were disappearing," she said. "You were trying to keep them safe."

The Guardian nodded slowly. "But without my true head, I cannot fulfill my duty. The harvest is at risk."

"We need to help him," Mia said, turning to her friends. "If we find his real head, we can stop the pumpkins from disappearing and save the festival."

"But where do we even start looking?" Jake asked, still a bit unsure.

Ella thought for a moment. "The sorcerer must have hidden the head somewhere nearby. Maybe there's a clue in the old stories. My grandma used to say that the sorcerer's lair was hidden in the darkest part of the woods, where the sun never shines."

"That's where we'll go," Mia decided. "We'll find the head and return it to the Guardian."

With the Guardian's directions, the trio ventured deeper into the woods, heading towards the darkest part of the forest. The trees grew thicker, their branches twisting like gnarled fingers. The air grew colder, and a thick fog began to rise from the ground.

Eventually, they came upon a hidden cave, its entrance covered in thick vines and moss. It was so dark inside that they could barely see, but Ella was prepared. She pulled out a small flashlight from her bag and led the way inside.

The cave was damp and eerie, with strange symbols carved into the walls. As they ventured further, they could hear the faint sound of dripping water echoing through the tunnels. The deeper they went, the more nervous they became, but they knew they couldn't turn back now.

Finally, they reached a large chamber at the heart of the cave. In the center of the room, surrounded by a circle of glowing runes, was a large, ancient pumpkin. It was dark and cracked, with an unmistakable aura of power. This had to be the Guardian's true head.

"There it is," Mia whispered, pointing to the pumpkin. "But how do we get it out of that circle?"

Ella studied the runes carefully. "These symbols are a binding spell," she explained. "The sorcerer must have used them to trap the head here. If we disrupt the circle, we can break the spell."

Jake, who had been unusually quiet, stepped forward. "I've got an idea," he said, picking up a large stick from the ground. He carefully reached over the glowing runes and tapped one of the symbols. The circle of light flickered and dimmed.

Encouraged, Mia and Ella joined in, using sticks to disrupt the other symbols. One by one, the runes faded until the circle was completely broken. The pumpkin head's glow brightened, and the kids could feel the magic in the air lift.

"It's working!" Ella exclaimed as the final rune vanished.

With the binding spell broken, the three friends carefully lifted the ancient pumpkin and made their way back through the cave and out into the forest. The journey back to the Guardian was faster now that they knew the way, and they soon found themselves in the clearing once again.

The Guardian's eyes lit up as they approached, holding his true head. "You have done it!" he rumbled, his voice filled with gratitude. "You have restored me!"

The kids gently placed the pumpkin head atop the Guardian's shoulders. As soon as it was in place, the vines and leaves of his body seemed to weave themselves together, and the cracks in the pumpkin head healed. The Guardian stood taller and stronger, his presence now full of power and protection.

"Thank you, brave ones," the Guardian said, his voice echoing with renewed strength. "The pumpkins are safe once more, and so is the harvest. As a token of my gratitude, you will always be welcome in this patch. The pumpkins will never be lost again."

The kids smiled, proud of what they had accomplished. The Guardian extended a vine and gently placed a glowing pumpkin seed in each of their hands.

"These seeds will grow into the finest pumpkins," he said. "May they remind you of your bravery and kindness."

23

The next day, the pumpkin patch was full and vibrant once again, with even more pumpkins than before. The townspeople marveled at the sudden abundance, but only Mia, Jake, and Ella knew the true story.

At the festival, the kids carved their pumpkins using the seeds given to them by the Guardian. Their jack-o'-lanterns glowed with an otherworldly light, and everyone who saw them was amazed by their brilliance.

As the sun set and the festival came to life with music, games, and laughter, the three friends shared a knowing smile. They had saved the pumpkins and the festival, and in doing so, they had become part of a secret that only they and the Guardian would ever know.

The mystery was solved, the pumpkins were safe, and the spirit of Halloween was stronger than ever in Willow Creek.

The Skeleton's Key

Oliver, Emily, and Max loved exploring old places in their town, especially when Halloween was around the corner. This year, they decided to check out the abandoned house at the edge of town, known as the Blackwood Manor. The house was rumored to be haunted, and no one had lived there for decades. The kids were both excited and a little scared as they approached the creaky, ivy-covered gate.

"Are we really doing this?" Max asked, glancing at the house with its broken windows and dark, looming shadows.

"Of course we are," Emily replied with a grin. "Think of all the stories we'll have to tell after this!"

Oliver nodded, feeling a mixture of nerves and curiosity. "Let's just make sure we stick together."

As they entered the house, it was like stepping back in time. Dust-covered furniture, cracked mirrors, and old paintings lined the walls. The floorboards creaked with every step they took. They explored room after room, finding nothing but cobwebs and old, forgotten trinkets.

But in one of the upstairs bedrooms, something caught Oliver's eye. On the dusty mantelpiece was a small, ornate box. He carefully opened it and found a key inside, made of old, tarnished silver and shaped like a skeleton.

"Guys, look at this!" Oliver said, holding up the key for Emily and Max to see.

"What do you think it opens?" Emily asked, intrigued.

"I don't know," Oliver replied. "But it's got to be important if it was hidden away like this."

Max, who was always up for an adventure, grinned. "Let's find out what it unlocks!"

With the key in hand, the kids searched the house for anything that might match the old, skeleton-shaped key. They tried it on doors, chests, and even a few old locks they found lying around, but nothing seemed to fit.

After what felt like hours of searching, they finally reached the last room in the house—the attic. The door was locked, and the keyhole looked different from the others they had tried.

"This has to be it," Emily said, her voice filled with excitement.

Oliver inserted the key into the lock, and with a soft click, the door swung open, revealing a dark, dusty attic filled with old furniture, trunks, and strange, shadowy shapes.

As they stepped inside, they noticed something unusual—a large wooden closet in the corner, standing slightly open. They cautiously approached it, their hearts pounding with anticipation.

Oliver slowly opened the closet door, and to their shock, a skeleton tumbled out, landing in a heap at their feet. It wasn't just any skeleton, though—it was wearing old, tattered clothes, and its bony fingers were clutching a piece of paper.

"What in the world...?" Max gasped, stepping back in surprise.

Emily, who was more curious than frightened, carefully took the paper from the skeleton's hand and unfolded it. It was a map, old and faded, with strange markings and a big red X in the center.

"This is a treasure map," she whispered, her eyes wide. "And I think this skeleton was trying to protect it."

The discovery of the map changed everything. The kids quickly forgot about their fear and focused on the possibility of finding hidden treasure. The map showed the layout of Blackwood Manor, with the X marking a spot deep within the house— somewhere they hadn't explored yet.

"It looks like the treasure is hidden in a secret room," Emily said, tracing the lines on the map with her finger. "We need to find it."

Using the map as their guide, the kids searched for any sign of a hidden door or passage. They checked behind paintings, under rugs, and even inside old cabinets. Finally, in the library, Max found something odd—a book on one of the shelves that didn't quite match the others. When he pulled it, the entire bookshelf slid aside, revealing a narrow staircase leading down into darkness.

"Found it!" Max called out, his voice echoing slightly in the narrow space.

With the key in hand, they descended the stairs into what appeared to be a hidden cellar. The air was cold and damp, and the walls were lined with shelves filled with ancient, dusty books. In the center of the room was a large, iron-bound chest, its lock shaped like a skeleton.

"This is it," Oliver said, holding up the key.

He inserted the key into the lock, and with a loud click, the chest opened. Inside, they found piles of gold coins, jewels, and old documents, all gleaming in the dim light of their flashlights.

"We found it!" Emily exclaimed, her eyes wide with excitement. "We found the treasure!"

But as they started to sift through the treasure, something strange began to happen. The air in the room grew colder, and a soft whispering sound filled the space.

The kids froze, realizing they weren't alone. Out of the shadows stepped a ghostly figure—the spirit of the skeleton they had found in the attic. It was translucent and glowing faintly, its eyes hollow and sad.

"Who dares disturb my rest?" the ghostly figure asked, its voice echoing with a mournful tone.

"We're sorry," Oliver said quickly. "We didn't mean to disturb you. We just found the key and followed the map."

The ghost's expression softened. "I see... I am the last of the Blackwood family. I was tasked with protecting this treasure, but I failed. The treasure was meant for those in need, but it has been forgotten, and so has my spirit."

Emily stepped forward, holding the map. "Maybe we can help you. If we take the treasure and use it for good, would that give you peace?"

The ghost seemed to consider this for a moment, then nodded. "Yes. If you use this treasure to help others, my spirit can finally rest."

Max, who had been quiet, spoke up. "We promise to do that. We'll make sure this treasure goes to those who need it."

The ghost smiled, a look of relief washing over its face. "Thank you. You have given me the peace I have long sought."

With that, the ghostly figure slowly faded away, leaving the kids alone with the treasure.

With the ghost at peace, the kids carefully gathered up the treasure and made their way back upstairs. They knew they had to keep their promise, so they decided to talk to the town's mayor and other leaders about using the treasure to help the community.

A few days later, on Halloween night, the entire town gathered for a special celebration. The mayor announced that a mysterious treasure had been found at Blackwood Manor and that it would be used to renovate the town's schools, build a new playground, and help families in need.

The townspeople cheered, and the kids felt a warm sense of pride, knowing they had done something truly special. As they looked out over the happy crowd, they thought they saw a faint, ghostly figure watching

34

from the shadows, smiling at them before disappearing into the night.

From that day on, the old Blackwood Manor was no longer seen as a haunted house but as a place of mystery and history, thanks to the bravery and kindness of three young friends who dared to explore its secrets.

The Costume Swap Curse

Lily and Sophie had been best friends for as long as they could remember. They did everything together—especially when it came to Halloween. This year, they were determined to have the best costumes at the annual Halloween party. Lily had chosen to dress as a glamorous vampire, complete with a flowing red cape and fangs, while Sophie decided on a spooky ghost, draped in an eerie, glowing white sheet.

On the afternoon of Halloween, they met at Sophie's house to put on their costumes and get ready for the party. The girls were excited as they helped each other with makeup, laughing and chatting about all the fun they were going to have.

"Do you think we'll win the costume contest?" Sophie asked, adjusting her ghostly sheet.

"Definitely!" Lily replied, showing off her sharp vampire fangs in the mirror. "No one else stands a chance."

They were just about to leave for the party when something strange happened. As they stood in front of the mirror admiring their costumes, a sudden gust of wind blew through the room, even though the windows were closed. The wind was strong enough to ruffle their costumes, and for a brief moment, everything around them seemed to shimmer and blur.

"What was that?" Lily asked, feeling a shiver run down her spine.

"I don't know," Sophie replied, equally unnerved. "It felt... weird."

Shrugging it off, they grabbed their bags and headed out the door, eager to show off their costumes. But neither of them noticed that something very strange had just taken place.

When they arrived at the party, everyone was already in high spirits. The music was playing, kids were bobbing for apples, and the room was filled with laughter and excitement. But as soon as Lily and Sophie walked in, they noticed something was off.

People began to stare at them—not in admiration, but in confusion. Some kids even gasped and whispered to each other, pointing at the girls with wide eyes.

"What's wrong with them?" Sophie whispered to Lily, feeling a bit self-conscious.

"I don't know," Lily replied, her confidence wavering. "Maybe they're just jealous of how great we look."

But when they reached the punch table, their friend Max looked at them with a puzzled expression. "Um, Lily... Sophie... why are you guys dressed like that?"

"Like what?" Lily asked, confused.

"Like actual ghosts and vampires," Max said, raising an eyebrow. "I mean, those costumes look really real."

Lily and Sophie exchanged confused glances. They were just about to laugh it off when they caught sight of their reflections in a nearby mirror. What they saw made their blood run cold.

Lily's reflection showed not a girl in a vampire costume, but an actual vampire—with pale skin, glowing red eyes, and sharp fangs that looked far too real. Sophie's reflection was even more shocking—she looked like a transparent, floating ghost, her once white sheet now a shimmering, otherworldly aura.

"What's happening to us?" Sophie cried, backing away from the mirror in terror.

"This isn't normal," Lily said, her voice trembling. "Something's gone terribly wrong."

Panicked, the girls rushed outside to try and figure out what had happened. As they stood in the cool night air, trying to calm down, they suddenly heard a pair of giggling voices. The laughter was eerie and seemed to come from all around them.

"Who's there?" Lily demanded, trying to sound brave.

Out of the shadows emerged two figures—ghostly twins with mischievous grins on their faces. They were identical in every way, with wispy white hair and eyes that gleamed with playful malice. They floated just above the ground, their translucent forms shimmering in the moonlight.

"Who are you?" Sophie asked, her voice shaking.

"We're the Trickster Twins," one of the spirits said with a smirk.

"And we love Halloween more than anything," the other added with a giggle.

"What did you do to us?" Lily demanded, trying to keep her fear in check.

"Oh, just a little costume swap," the first twin replied, twirling in the air. "You see, we were bored of being spirits, so we decided to have a bit of fun."

The second twin continued, "Now you're wearing our costumes, and we're wearing yours! Isn't it delightful?"

"Not really," Sophie said, feeling a chill run down her spine. "How do we undo it?"

The Trickster Twins exchanged glances and then smiled. "That's the fun part—you have until midnight to find us and reverse the swap. Otherwise..."

"Otherwise what?" Lily asked, dreading the answer.

"Otherwise, you'll stay like this forever," the twins chimed in unison, their voices full of mischief.

With that, the Trickster Twins vanished into thin air, their laughter echoing through the night.

Lily and Sophie were left standing in the empty street, feeling more terrified than they had ever felt in their lives. They had to reverse the curse, but they had no idea where to start.

"We have to find them," Sophie said, her voice shaking. "We can't let this happen. We can't turn into real ghosts and vampires!"

"But how do we find spirits that can disappear at will?" Lily asked, starting to panic. "We don't even know where they went!"

Just then, Max, who had followed them outside, approached cautiously. "Hey, are you guys okay? I heard everything."

"No, we're not okay!" Lily snapped, before taking a deep breath. "Sorry, Max, it's just... we don't know what to do."

Max thought for a moment. "Maybe they're hiding somewhere they think is fun. The twins sound like they love Halloween, so maybe they're at a place with a lot of Halloween spirit."

Sophie's eyes lit up. "The haunted house! The one on Elm Street where they do that big Halloween attraction every year!"

"Of course!" Lily said, hope flooding back. "If we're going to find them anywhere, it's there."

With Max's help, the girls raced across town to the haunted house. The streets were filled with trick-or-treaters and Halloween decorations, but they had no time to lose. The clock was ticking toward midnight.

The haunted house was packed with people, all enjoying the spooky attractions. Lily and Sophie pushed through the crowds, searching every corner for the Trickster Twins. The house was full of creepy decorations, jump scares, and eerie sound effects, making their search even more nerve-wracking.

As they passed through a hall of mirrors, something caught Sophie's eye. In the reflection of one mirror, she saw the Trickster Twins, their ghostly forms flickering in and out of sight.

"There they are!" Sophie shouted, grabbing Lily's hand.

They rushed into the mirror maze, where the Trickster Twins were waiting for them, giggling mischievously.

"Ready to swap back?" one twin asked, floating just out of reach.

"You have to catch us first!" the other twin taunted.

The girls darted after the twins, but the mirror maze made everything confusing. The reflections bounced off the walls, making it hard to tell where the real Trickster Twins were. Every time they thought they had them cornered, the twins would slip away, laughing all the while.

But as the clock in the town square began to chime, signaling that midnight was only minutes away, Lily had an idea.

"Let's use the mirrors against them," she whispered to Sophie. "If we break the reflections, they'll have nowhere to hide!"

Working together, the girls blocked the Trickster Twins into a corner of the maze. Sophie quickly used her ghostly form to pass through a mirror, surprising the twins from behind. With a final push, Lily used her vampire strength to block their escape.

"Alright, you win!" the twins said, holding up their hands in surrender. "We'll swap back."

As the last chime of midnight sounded, the Trickster Twins waved their hands, and a swirl of magic surrounded Lily and Sophie. In an instant, the girls were back to their normal selves, standing in their original costumes.

"Thank you!" Sophie said, feeling more like herself again.

The twins, now visible only in the mirrors, gave them a mischievous grin. "You were fun to play with. Maybe we'll see you again next Halloween."

And with that, the Trickster Twins vanished, leaving only their laughter behind.

Relieved and exhausted, Lily and Sophie made their way back to the Halloween party. They were just in time for the costume contest, and though they didn't win, they didn't care. They had their own story to tell, one that was more exciting and spooky than any costume could ever be.

As the night wound down, they sat with Max, laughing and sharing candy, grateful that the curse had been lifted.

"Next year," Lily said with a grin, "let's stick to less magical costumes."

Sophie laughed. "Agreed. But I have to admit, that was the most memorable Halloween ever."

The three friends smiled, knowing that this Halloween would be one they would never forget.

The Witch's Candy Cauldron

Timmy was an ordinary boy with a sweet tooth, and Halloween was his favorite time of year. He loved dressing up, trick-or-treating, and—most of all—eating candy. This year, however, he wanted something more than just a bag of sweets. Timmy wanted something extraordinary.

One chilly October evening, as he wandered through the neighborhood looking for new places to trick-or-treat, he stumbled upon a strange little shop that he had never noticed before. The shop's sign, written in crooked, glowing letters, read "Morgana's Magical Sweets."

Intrigued, Timmy pushed open the creaky door and stepped inside. The shop was dimly lit, with shelves full of jars and boxes that contained the most unusual candies he had ever seen. The air smelled of caramel, chocolate, and something else—something magical.

Behind the counter stood an old woman with wild, silver hair and a pointy hat. She had a mischievous smile on her face as she watched Timmy explore the shop.

"Looking for something special, are we?" the woman asked in a raspy voice.

Timmy hesitated, feeling a bit nervous under her gaze. "Yeah, I guess so. Something different for Halloween."

The woman's eyes twinkled. "I have just the thing." She reached under the counter and pulled out a small, bubbling cauldron filled with colorful candies. "This is Morgana's Candy Cauldron. Every piece of candy inside grants a wish, but be careful—each wish comes with a price."

Timmy's eyes widened. "A wish-granting candy? That's awesome!"

The witch cackled softly. "Indeed it is. But remember, not everything is as sweet as it seems. Choose wisely."

Without thinking much of the warning, Timmy paid for the cauldron and hurried home, eager to try out his new magical candies.

As soon as Timmy got home, he placed the cauldron on his desk and peered inside. The candies looked like ordinary sweets—brightly colored gumdrops, lollipops, and chocolates. But Timmy knew they were anything but ordinary.

"What should I wish for first?" he wondered aloud, his mind racing with possibilities.

He decided to start small. "I wish for the biggest, most delicious candy bar in the world!"

He picked a shiny, red candy from the cauldron and popped it into his mouth. The moment he swallowed it, there was a flash of light, and in his hands appeared a massive candy bar, bigger than any he had ever seen. It was wrapped in golden foil and smelled of rich chocolate.

"Wow!" Timmy exclaimed, tearing open the wrapper. But as soon as he took a bite, something strange happened. The chocolate was delicious, but it was so sticky that it glued his mouth shut. He tried to speak, but no words came out. He could only mumble in panic as he realized he couldn't open his mouth at all!

Terrified, Timmy ran to the mirror and saw that his lips were sealed shut with a thick layer of sticky chocolate. He couldn't scream, he couldn't talk—he could barely breathe!

Desperate, he ran back to the cauldron and quickly scribbled on a piece of paper: "I wish for my mouth to be free!"

He grabbed another candy and swallowed it, praying it would work. Instantly, the chocolate melted away, and he could speak again. He gasped for air, clutching his throat in relief.

"That was close," Timmy muttered. "I've got to be more careful with these wishes."

But the lure of the candy cauldron was too strong to resist. Even though his first wish had gone wrong, Timmy couldn't help but think about all the other amazing things he could wish for.

The next day at school, Timmy couldn't stop thinking about the cauldron. During recess, his friend Jack was showing off his new bike, bragging about how fast it was and how everyone wanted one just like it. Timmy felt a twinge of jealousy.

"I wish I had the coolest bike in the world," Timmy thought to himself as he reached into his pocket and pulled out a small, green candy he had taken from the cauldron.

He quickly popped the candy into his mouth and waited. Sure enough, by the time he got home, a brand-new bike was waiting for him on the front lawn. It was sleek, shiny, and unlike any bike he had ever seen. The wheels had glowing lights, the handlebars were covered in polished metal, and the seat was cushioned with plush leather.

"This is amazing!" Timmy shouted, hopping onto the bike.

But as soon as he started pedaling, the bike took off at an incredible speed. It was as if it had a mind of its own, zooming down the street faster than Timmy could control. He tried to brake, but the bike wouldn't stop. It sped around corners, swerved through traffic, and jumped over curbs. Timmy was terrified, gripping the handlebars for dear life.

"Stop! Stop!" he shouted, but the bike only seemed to go faster.

Just as he thought he might crash, the bike suddenly skidded to a halt in front of his house, tossing him onto the grass. Timmy's heart was pounding, and he was covered in scrapes and bruises.

"That was way too close," he muttered, limping back into the house.

Timmy realized that every wish he made was getting more dangerous.

The candy cauldron wasn't just granting his wishes—it was testing him, challenging him to think before he acted.

Determined to be more careful, Timmy decided to try one last wish. This time, he would think it through. Halloween was only a day away, and he still didn't have a costume. He wanted something unique, something that would make him stand out at the Halloween party.

"I wish for the most amazing Halloween costume ever," Timmy said carefully as he selected a purple candy from the cauldron.

Instantly, a shimmering costume appeared on his bed. It was a wizard's robe, complete with a pointy hat, glowing runes, and a staff that crackled with magical energy. Timmy couldn't believe his luck. The costume was perfect.

But as soon as he put it on, something strange happened. The runes on the robe began to glow brighter, and the staff sparked with real electricity. Timmy felt a surge of power rush through him, and before he knew it, he was floating off the ground.

"What's happening?" he cried out, trying to get his feet back on the floor.

But the costume had a mind of its own. Timmy was pulled out the window, soaring through the sky like a real wizard. At first, it was thrilling—flying over rooftops and trees, casting sparks of light from the staff. But then the costume started to take him higher and higher, beyond the clouds, where the air grew thin and cold.

Panicking, Timmy realized he had no control over where he was going. The costume was dragging him away, far from home, and he couldn't stop it.

Desperately, he reached into his pocket and pulled out a final candy from the cauldron—a blue one he had saved just in case. With trembling hands, he made a wish.

"I wish to be safely back home!"

In a flash, Timmy was back in his bedroom, lying on the floor in his normal clothes. The wizard costume was gone, and so was the cauldron, which had disappeared along with the last wish.

As Halloween night arrived, Timmy didn't have a fancy costume or magical candy. Instead, he put on a simple pirate costume he had worn the previous year and went trick-or-treating with his friends.

When they asked him why he didn't have a new costume this year, Timmy just smiled and shrugged. "Sometimes, it's better to stick with what you know," he said.

That Halloween, Timmy enjoyed the night like never before. He realized that he didn't need magical wishes to have fun or be happy. In fact, he was glad to be just an ordinary boy, with ordinary candy and ordinary friends.

As he lay in bed that night, he thought about the witch and her candy cauldron. Maybe she had known all along that he needed to learn a lesson about being careful with his wishes. Timmy promised himself that he would never take anything for granted again—especially not something that seemed too good to be true.

And as he drifted off to sleep, he heard a faint, mischievous cackle in the wind, as if the witch was watching over him, pleased that he had finally learned his lesson.

The Midnight Monster Parade

In the small town of Shadowville, every child knew the legend of the Midnight Monster Parade. It was said that on Halloween night, when the clock struck midnight, the monsters of the town would come out for a grand parade. But there was a catch—only the bravest children who stayed up until midnight and faced their deepest fears could see the parade.

For years, no one had ever actually seen the parade. Some said it was just a silly old story, while others claimed they had heard strange noises or caught glimpses of shadows moving in the dark. But no one had ever stayed up long enough to prove it.

This Halloween, Lily and her younger brother Max decided that they would be the ones to finally witness the Midnight Monster Parade. They had heard the stories from their grandparents and their friends, and they were determined to see it for themselves.

"Are you sure we should do this?" Max asked nervously as they prepared for bed that night. He was only seven, and while he loved Halloween, the thought of real monsters gave him the creeps.

"Of course, we should!" Lily replied, her eyes shining with excitement. She was nine and loved adventure. "Think about how cool it would be to tell everyone that we saw the parade. We'll be the first ones ever!"

Max wasn't entirely convinced, but he didn't want to disappoint his sister. So, they made a pact: they would stay up together, no matter what, and watch the Midnight Monster Parade.

Lily and Max made their preparations carefully. They set up camp in the living room, with blankets, pillows, and a stash of Halloween candy to keep them awake. Their parents thought it was just part of the Halloween fun and didn't suspect that the siblings had any serious plans to stay up until midnight.

As the hours ticked by, the house grew quiet. Their parents went to bed, and the streets outside became still, with only the occasional rustle of leaves in the wind. Lily and Max played games, told spooky stories, and ate their candy, but as the night wore on, Max began to feel sleepy.

"Maybe the parade isn't real," Max yawned, his eyes drooping. "Maybe we should just go to bed."

But Lily wasn't giving up. "Come on, Max! We're so close. Just think about all those monsters parading down the street—don't you want to see that?"

Max nodded, trying to keep his eyes open. He wanted to be brave like Lily, but he couldn't shake the feeling that something scary might happen if they stayed up.

Finally, the clock struck eleven. Only one hour to go.

As they waited, a sudden noise made them both jump. It was a soft scratching sound, like something was moving outside the window.

"What was that?" Max whispered, clutching his blanket.

Lily tried to sound brave. "Probably just the wind. Or a raccoon."

But the scratching continued, growing louder. Max's heart pounded as he looked at the window. "What if it's a monster?"

Lily swallowed hard. "Only one way to find out."

With trembling hands, she crept to the window and peeked outside. The yard was dark, with only the faint glow of the moon illuminating the trees. But as her eyes adjusted, she saw something moving—a shadowy figure, crawling across the ground.

"It's...it's coming closer!" Lily gasped, her voice shaking.

Max hid behind her, too scared to move. "What do we do?"

Lily took a deep breath. "We have to face it. Remember, we have to be brave if we want to see the parade."

Gathering all her courage, Lily opened the window. The cold night air rushed in, carrying with it the sound of the scratching. And then, they saw it—a small, furry creature with glowing eyes.

"It's a raccoon!" Lily exclaimed, laughing in relief.

The raccoon looked at them curiously, then scurried away into the bushes. Max let out a sigh of relief, but his legs were still shaky.

"That was scary," he admitted.

"But we faced it," Lily said, giving him a reassuring smile. "And we're still here. Let's keep going."

As midnight approached, the air seemed to grow colder, and the house became eerily quiet. Lily and Max huddled together, their excitement mingled with nervousness. They had faced their first fear, but what else was waiting for them?

The clock ticked closer to twelve, and just as the final minute was about to pass, a strange noise echoed through the house. It was a low, rumbling growl, coming from the direction of the basement.

Max's face went pale. "What was that?"

Lily's heart raced. "I...I don't know. But we can't stop now."

Holding hands, they tiptoed toward the basement door. The growling grew louder, more menacing. Max squeezed Lily's hand so tightly that it hurt, but she didn't let go.

When they reached the basement door, they hesitated. The growling was so close now, it felt like whatever was making the noise was right on the other side.

"Are you ready?" Lily asked, her voice barely a whisper.

Max nodded, though his knees were shaking. "Let's do it."

With a deep breath, Lily opened the door. The growling stopped instantly, and they were greeted by complete silence. The basement was pitch black, with only the faintest light coming from the top of the stairs.

But then, something moved in the darkness. A shadowy figure loomed at the bottom of the stairs, tall and hulking, its eyes glowing a sickly green.

Max froze in terror. "L-Lily..."

Lily felt her own fear rising, but she knew they had come too far to back out now. "We have to be brave," she whispered. "For the parade."

Steeling herself, she stepped forward, pulling Max with her. The shadowy figure didn't move, but the growling started again, louder and more menacing than before.

Lily's heart was pounding so hard she thought it might burst. But as she took another step, something incredible happened. The figure began to fade, and the growling turned into a low, rumbling laugh.

Suddenly, the basement was filled with a soft, eerie light, and the shadowy figure transformed into a ghostly old man, his face kind but mischievous.

"Congratulations, children," the ghostly man said in a deep, echoing voice. "You have proven your bravery."

Lily and Max stared in shock, unable to believe what they were seeing. The ghostly man smiled at them, his eyes twinkling with amusement.

"The Midnight Monster Parade awaits," he said, extending his hand toward them. "Come, join the fun."

As the ghostly man led them outside, Lily and Max could hardly contain their excitement. The street, once empty and quiet, was now filled with creatures of all shapes and sizes.

There were werewolves howling at the moon, vampires with capes billowing in the wind, witches on broomsticks cackling in the air, and skeletons dancing to the beat of ghostly drums.

The monsters marched in a grand parade, their costumes vibrant and their faces filled with joy. It was a sight unlike anything Lily and Max had ever imagined. And the best part? The monsters weren't scary at all. They were friendly, waving and smiling at the two children as they passed by.

Lily and Max joined in, dancing and laughing alongside the monsters. They twirled with the ghosts, played tag with the werewolves, and shared candy with the vampires. It was the most magical night of their lives.

As the parade wound down, the ghostly man appeared again, tipping his hat to them. "You have done well, brave ones. The Midnight Monster

Parade is a reward for those who dare to face their fears. Remember this night, and know that courage will always be rewarded."

With a final wave, the ghostly man disappeared, and the monsters began to fade away, returning to the shadows from which they came.

Lily and Max stood in the quiet street, the only sound being the soft rustle of leaves in the wind. They smiled at each other, knowing they had shared something special—something that no one else in Shadowville had ever experienced.

As they walked back to their house, Max looked up at Lily and said, "That was the best Halloween ever."

Lily nodded, her heart full of pride and joy. "It really was. And we'll always have the Midnight Monster Parade to remind us how brave we can be."

And with that, they went inside, ready to finally rest after the most exciting Halloween night of their lives.

The Magic Broom Ride

Ella was a young witch-in-training, and this Halloween was a very special night for her. It was the night she would take her first solo broom ride, something she had been eagerly anticipating for months. Ella had practiced in her backyard, flying low to the ground under the watchful eye of her mother, but tonight was different. Tonight, she would soar into the skies all by herself.

Dressed in her favorite purple robe, with her pointed hat slightly askew, Ella held her broom tightly as she prepared to take off from her front yard. The full moon shone brightly, casting a silvery glow over the neighborhood. Excitement bubbled in her chest as she muttered the takeoff spell her mother had taught her.

"Up, up, and away!"

The broom lifted off the ground, wobbled for a moment, and then steadied as Ella found her balance. With a delighted giggle, she soared higher into the air, leaving the familiar sights of her house and street below.

As she flew over the neighborhood, Ella marveled at the sights of Halloween night. Children in costumes ran from house to house, collecting candy in their treat bags. The houses were decorated with glowing jack-o'-lanterns, spooky skeletons, and cobwebs. The air was filled with the sound of laughter and the occasional howl of a fake werewolf.

But as she rounded a corner, something unexpected happened. Ella's broom gave a sudden lurch, and she felt it dip toward the ground. Before she could regain control, the broom swooped down and, to her surprise, scooped up three neighborhood kids who were out trick-or-treating.

The kids, dressed as a pirate, a ghost, and a superhero, let out yelps of surprise as they found themselves lifted off the ground and zooming through the air. Ella, equally startled, looked down at them with wide eyes.

"What are you doing on my broom?" she exclaimed, trying to steady the ride.

"We didn't mean to!" shouted the boy dressed as a pirate, his plastic sword flapping in the wind. "It just grabbed us!"

"I think it's enchanted!" said the girl dressed as a ghost, her white sheet billowing like a sail.

"Whoa, this is awesome!" cheered the superhero, clearly enjoying the ride despite the confusion.

Ella realized her broom must have sensed the children's presence and had acted on its own to bring them along. But now, with three extra passengers, the broom was becoming harder to control. It swayed and dipped, heading straight for a group of tall trees.

"Hang on!" Ella shouted as she tried to steer the broom away from the trees.

The broom barely missed the treetops, and the kids held on tightly, their initial fear turning into excitement. This wasn't a regular Halloween anymore—this was a real adventure!

As Ella tried to figure out how to safely return the kids to the ground, the broom suddenly took a sharp turn, leading them out of the neighborhood and into a part of the sky that shimmered with a strange, magical light.

The night around them changed. The sky deepened into a velvety blackness, dotted with twinkling stars that seemed closer than ever. The moon grew larger and more luminous, and beneath them, the landscape transformed into something entirely different. Gone were the familiar houses and streets. In their place were dark, mysterious forests, bubbling swamps, and winding paths that led to unknown destinations.

"Where are we?" asked the superhero, his voice filled with awe.

"This is the magical world of Halloween," Ella said, her voice tinged with both wonder and concern. "It's where all the Halloween creatures live—witches, goblins, ghosts, and more. I didn't mean to bring us here!"

The broom seemed to have a mind of its own, carrying them deeper into the magical world. They flew over a witch's market, where cauldrons bubbled with strange potions and black cats prowled around stalls selling enchanted items. They passed a haunted forest, where ghostly figures floated between the trees, and a pumpkin patch with giant jack-o'-lanterns that grinned and winked at them.

"This is incredible!" said the ghost, her eyes wide with amazement. "But how do we get back?"

Ella bit her lip, unsure of how to answer. She had only meant to go on a short flight, not an entire adventure through the magical realms. But she knew one thing—if they didn't find their way back before sunrise, they might be stuck here until the next Halloween.

Determined to get the kids home safely, Ella tried to take control of the broom again. But it seemed the magical world had other plans. The broom dipped and swerved, leading them toward a spooky castle perched on a hill. The castle was surrounded by bats and glowing orbs of light, and its windows flickered with eerie green flames.

As they approached, the broom slowed down, hovering near the entrance of the castle. The large wooden doors creaked open on their own, inviting them inside.

"We can't go in there!" said the pirate, his voice shaking a little. "It looks too scary!"

"But maybe there's someone inside who can help us," said Ella, trying to sound brave. She knew that time was running out—they had to find a way home before sunrise.

With a deep breath, Ella guided the broom into the castle. The inside was just as spooky as the outside, with dark hallways, cobwebs hanging from the ceiling, and strange shadows moving in the corners. The kids huddled close to Ella, their earlier excitement now mixed with nervousness.

At the end of a long corridor, they found themselves in a grand hall with a high ceiling and a large chandelier made of bones. In the center of the room stood a tall figure dressed in dark robes, his face hidden by a hood.

"Welcome, young witch," the figure said in a deep, echoing voice. "And welcome to your friends. What brings you to my castle on this Halloween night?"

Ella swallowed hard. "We didn't mean to come here. My broom brought us by accident, and now we need to find our way home before sunrise."

The hooded figure nodded slowly. "Ah, I see. You've entered the magical world of Halloween, where time and space are not what they seem. But fear not—I can help you return. However, you must complete a task first."

"What kind of task?" asked the superhero, his voice steady despite the eerie surroundings.

The figure raised a hand, and a glowing map appeared in the air. "You must find the three enchanted pumpkins that are hidden within this world. Each pumpkin holds a piece of the spell that will return you to your world. But be warned—the pumpkins are guarded by creatures of the night. You'll need courage and cleverness to retrieve them."

Ella and the kids exchanged determined looks. They had come this far—they weren't going to back down now.

"We'll do it," Ella said, her voice firm.

The hooded figure handed her the map, and with a wave of his hand, the doors of the castle swung open once more.

"Good luck," he said. "And remember—time is of the essence."

The broom carried them back into the night, the glowing map guiding their way. The first pumpkin was hidden in the haunted forest, guarded by a group of mischievous ghosts. The forest was dark and filled with eerie noises, but the kids knew they had to be brave. They worked together to outsmart the ghosts, using their costumes and quick thinking to distract them long enough for Ella to grab the pumpkin.

The second pumpkin was in the pumpkin patch thcy had passcd earlier, guarded by giant jack-o'-lanterns that came to life when they tried to take the enchanted one. The kids used their agility and teamwork to dodge the grinning pumpkins, finally managing to retrieve the enchanted one with a well-timed distraction.

The final pumpkin was the trickiest. It was hidden in the witch's market, guarded by a powerful witch who wasn't keen on giving it up. But Ella, with her own budding magic, managed to strike a deal with the witch, trading one of her own Halloween treats for the pumpkin.

With all three pumpkins in hand, the kids and Ella hurried back to the castle. The hooded figure was waiting for them, his dark robes billowing as they approached.

"Very well done," he said, his voice filled with approval. "Now, the spell."

He combined the three pumpkins, and they glowed with a bright light. The air around them shimmered, and the castle began to fade. The kids and Ella felt a swirling sensation as they were lifted off the ground and carried through the magical world, back to the neighborhood they had left behind.

With a soft thud, the broom landed back in the neighborhood, just as the first light of dawn began to peek over the horizon. The kids looked around in amazement—they were back home, safe and sound.

"We did it!" the pirate cheered, punching the air with his plastic sword.

Ella smiled, relief flooding through her. She had managed to keep the kids safe and complete her first solo broom ride, even if it had turned out to be much more adventurous than she had planncd.

"Thank you, Ella," the ghost said, giving her a big hug. "That was the best Halloween ever!"

"You're welcome," Ella replied, returning the hug. "I'm just glad we all made it back."

As the kids hurried off to their homes, Ella watched them go with a smile. She knew this Halloween would be one she'd never forget, and she couldn't wait to tell her mother all about the magical world she had discovered.

With a final wave to her new friends, Ella took off on her broom once more, the morning breeze ruffling her hair as she headed home, ready for whatever new adventures the next Halloween might bring.

The Monster Under the Bed

Max had always been a little afraid of the dark. Especially at night when the lights went out, and the shadows seemed to grow bigger and creepier. But what scared him the most was the idea that there might be something lurking under his bed.

Every night, before he went to sleep, Max would peek under the bed, just to make sure there was nothing there. And every night, he'd find the same thing—dust bunnies, an old sock, and a couple of lost toys. But one night, something strange happened.

As Max was lying in bed, trying to fall asleep, he heard a soft shuffling sound. At first, he thought it was just the wind rustling outside, but then he heard it again. It was coming from under his bed.

Max's heart pounded in his chest. He pulled the covers up to his chin and squeezed his eyes shut, hoping that whatever it was would just go away. But the noise didn't stop. In fact, it sounded like it was getting closer.

"Who's there?" Max whispered, his voice trembling.

To his surprise, a quiet voice answered, "I'm sorry if I scared you. I didn't mean to."

Max's eyes flew open, and he stared at the dark space under his bed. "Who are you?" he asked, still frightened but also a little curious.

There was a pause, and then a small, furry head poked out from under the bed. The creature had big, round eyes that glowed softly in the dark and a pair of floppy ears. It was definitely a monster, but it didn't look as scary as Max had imagined.

"My name's Fizzle," the creature said shyly. "I live under your bed."

Max blinked in surprise. "You're a real monster?"

Fizzle nodded. "Yes, but I'm not a scary monster. At least, I try not to be."

Max felt a mix of relief and amazement. He had always thought that if there was a monster under his bed, it would be big and terrifying. But Fizzle was small, with a round, fuzzy body and a nervous smile.

"Why do you live under my bed?" Max asked, sitting up in bed.

"It's a good hiding place," Fizzle said, shrugging his tiny shoulders. "Most kids are too scared to look under there, so it's safe for me. But I didn't mean to scare you. I just wanted to see if you were nice."

Max felt his fear melting away. "I'm not scared of you," he said, offering Fizzle a small smile. "But why would you want to hide from me?"

Fizzle hesitated, then confessed, "Well... I'm a little scared of humans. They're big and loud, and they always scream when they see me. But you didn't scream, so I think you're different."

Max was surprised. He had never thought that a monster could be afraid of humans. "I'm not going to hurt you," he said gently. "Maybe we could be friends?"

Fizzle's eyes lit up. "Really? You'd want to be friends with a monster?"

Max nodded. "Sure! Besides, you don't seem like a scary monster at all."

Fizzle beamed with joy. "Thank you! You're the first human who's ever said that."

As the night went on, Max and Fizzle talked about all sorts of things. Max told Fizzle about his school, his friends, and his favorite toys. In return, Fizzle shared stories about his world—a place full of other monsters, where the sky was always a deep shade of purple and the trees had leaves that glowed in the dark.

"Would you like to see it?" Fizzle asked excitedly. "I could show you around!"

Max's eyes widened. "You mean I could come with you to your world?"

Fizzle nodded eagerly. "Yes! It's not far, and it's not as scary as you might think. There are lots of friendly monsters there, just like me."

Max hesitated for a moment. He had never been to another world before, and the idea of visiting a place full of monsters made him a little nervous. But Fizzle seemed so friendly and excited that Max couldn't resist the offer.

"Okay," Max said, taking a deep breath. "Let's go!"

Fizzle's face lit up with excitement. "Great! Just hold onto my hand, and I'll take you there."

Max climbed out of bed and reached for Fizzle's furry hand. As soon as their hands touched, a soft glow surrounded them, and the room began to spin. Max felt a strange sensation, like he was being lifted off the ground, and before he knew it, they were floating in a swirling tunnel of light.

When the spinning stopped, Max found himself standing in a completely different place. The sky was a deep purple, just as Fizzle had described, and the ground beneath his feet was soft and spongy. The trees around them had glowing leaves that cast a gentle light on the path ahead.

"Welcome to my world!" Fizzle said, spreading his arms wide. "What do you think?"

Max looked around in awe. "It's amazing! I've never seen anything like it."

Fizzle grinned. "I'm glad you like it. Come on, I'll show you around."

As they walked along the glowing path, Max saw all sorts of strange and wonderful creatures. There were monsters of all shapes and sizes—some with long, wiggly arms, others with multiple eyes, and a few that looked like they were made of clouds. But despite their unusual appearances, none of the monsters seemed scary. In fact, most of them smiled and waved as they passed by.

"Hi, Fizzle!" called a tall, thin monster with a long neck and a hat perched on top of its head. "Who's your friend?"

"This is Max," Fizzle replied proudly. "He's a human!"

The tall monster's eyes widened in surprise. "A human? Wow! I've never met one before."

"Don't worry, Max is nice," Fizzle assured the tall monster. "He's not scary at all."

Max smiled and waved back, feeling more at ease with each step. The more monsters he met, the more he realized that they were just like Fizzle— friendly, kind, and a little shy around humans.

As they continued their journey, Fizzle introduced Max to some of his monster friends. There was Blinky, a small, round monster with eyes that blinked in different colors; Puff, a fluffy monster who loved to sing; and Sprocket, a mechanical monster who could build just about anything with his collection of gears and tools.

Max was having so much fun that he almost forgot he was in a world full of monsters. Everyone was so welcoming and friendly that it felt like he had known them all his life.

As the night went on, Max noticed that Fizzle seemed a little quieter than before. He wasn't as cheerful as he had been when they first arrived, and Max could tell that something was bothering him.

"Are you okay, Fizzle?" Max asked, concerned.

Fizzle hesitated, then sighed. "It's just... I'm glad you're here, Max, but there's something I'm scared of, and I don't know how to face it."

Max was surprised. "What are you scared of? You seem so brave."

Fizzle shook his head. "I'm not as brave as you think. There's a part of our world that I've always been afraid to visit. It's called the Shadow Valley, and it's where the scariest monsters live. I've heard stories about it, but I've never been there myself."

Max thought for a moment. He knew what it was like to be scared of the unknown—he had been afraid of the dark and the monster under his bed, after all. But now that he knew Fizzle, he realized that sometimes things weren't as scary as they seemed.

"What if we went together?" Max suggested. "Maybe it won't be as scary if we face it together."

Fizzle looked at Max in surprise. "You'd do that? Even though it's really scary?"

Max nodded. "You helped me face my fear of monsters. Now I want to help you face your fear."

Fizzle smiled, feeling a little braver with Max by his side. "Okay. Let's go."

The journey to the Shadow Valley was long and filled with strange noises that made Fizzle shiver. But with Max by his side, he kept going. When they finally reached the entrance to the valley, they stopped and looked at the dark, misty landscape ahead.

The valley was filled with twisted trees, and the shadows seemed to move on their own. It was a place that would have scared Max before, but now, with Fizzle's hand in his, he felt a surge of courage.

"Let's go," Max said, taking a step forward.

As they walked through the valley, they saw shadowy figures moving in the distance. Fizzle's hand trembled, but he kept going, determined to face his fear.

Finally, they reached the heart of the valley, where the scariest monster of all was said to live. But when they arrived, they found something unexpected. The monster wasn't a big, terrifying creature—it was a small, lonely monster with large, sad eyes.

The monster looked up at them, surprised to see visitors. "Who are you?" it asked in a quiet voice.

"I'm Fizzle, and this is my friend Max," Fizzle replied, his fear slowly melting away. "We came here because we were scared, but now we see that you're just like us."

The lonely monster blinked in surprise. "You're not afraid of me?"

Max shook his head. "No. We were scared at first, but we've learned that things aren't always as scary as they seem."

The monster smiled, a little tear rolling down its cheek. "Thank you. I've been alone for so long because everyone is afraid of me. But I'm not scary—I'm just different."

Max and Fizzle sat down with the monster, and they talked for a long time. By the end of the night, they had made a new friend, and the Shadow Valley didn't seem so scary anymore.

When Max and Fizzle finally returned to Max's room, the sun was just starting to rise. Max yawned, feeling sleepy but happy. He had made new friends, faced his fears, and discovered that monsters weren't so different from humans after all.

"Thank you for coming with me, Max," Fizzle said, giving Max a hug. "You helped me be brave."

Max smiled and hugged Fizzle back. "And you helped me too. I'm not afraid of the dark anymore."

As Max climbed back into bed, Fizzle gave him a final wave before disappearing under the bed. Max knew that Fizzle would always be there, not as a scary monster, but as a friend.

From that night on, Max never felt afraid of the dark again. And whenever he heard a soft shuffling sound under his bed, he smiled, knowing that his friend Fizzle was close by, ready for their next adventure.

Ghost in the Library

Lena loved the library. It was her favorite place in the world, where she could escape into the pages of a good book and let her imagination run wild. Every Saturday, Lena would spend hours in the library, exploring different sections and discovering new stories.

But there was one section of the library that always intrigued her—the Old Book Room. It was tucked away in the back, behind a heavy wooden door that creaked whenever someone opened it. The books in that room were ancient, their pages yellowed with age, and the air was thick with the scent of old paper.

One rainy afternoon, Lena decided to visit the Old Book Room. She pushed open the door and stepped inside, feeling a chill in the air. The room was dimly lit, and the shelves were crammed with books of all shapes and sizes. Most people avoided this room because it was so dusty and dark, but to Lena, it felt like a treasure trove of forgotten stories.

As she wandered through the narrow aisles, Lena noticed a book lying open on a small table. It looked out of place, as if someone had just been reading it. Curious, she walked over to the table and peered at the open pages.

The book was titled *The Ghost of the Library*, and the illustration on the first page showed a shadowy figure floating among the bookshelves. Lena felt a shiver run down her spine, but she couldn't help herself—she had to know more.

She sat down at the table and began to read. The story was about a librarian who had dedicated her life to taking care of the library and its books. But after she passed away, her spirit couldn't rest because there was something she hadn't finished. Now, her ghost haunted the library, searching for someone who could help her complete her final task.

Lena was so engrossed in the story that she didn't notice the temperature in the room drop. The air grew colder, and a faint rustling sound filled the room. When Lena finally looked up, she gasped.

Standing before her was a translucent figure—a woman with kind eyes and a gentle smile. She was dressed in an old-fashioned librarian's uniform, and she looked exactly like the ghost in the book.

"Don't be afraid," the ghost said in a soft voice. "I'm not here to harm you."

Lena's heart raced, but she managed to nod. "Are you... the ghost from the story?"

The ghost nodded. "Yes. My name is Mrs. Grimsby. I was the librarian here many years ago. I've been waiting for someone like you—someone who loves books as much as I do."

Lena's fear began to fade, replaced by curiosity. "What do you need help with?"

Mrs. Grimsby's expression grew serious. "There is one book in this library that was never returned. It's the last book I lent out before I passed away. I can't rest until it's back on the shelf where it belongs."

Lena's eyes widened. "Do you know where the book is?"

The ghost shook her head. "I've searched every corner of the library, but I can't find it. That's why I need your help. Will you help me find the missing book?"

Lena didn't hesitate. "Yes, I'll help you. Where do we start?"

Mrs. Grimsby smiled gratefully. "Thank you, dear. The book was titled *The Lost Tale of Hollow Hill*. It's a very old, very special book. I lent it to a young boy who never returned it. I believe it might still be somewhere in the library, hidden away."

Lena nodded, determined to solve the mystery. "Let's find it."

Lena and Mrs. Grimsby began their search in the Old Book Room. They carefully checked each shelf, pulling out books and flipping through their pages, but there was no sign of *The Lost Tale of Hollow Hill*.

"This book must be well-hidden," Mrs. Grimsby mused, floating beside Lena. "The boy who borrowed it was very shy. He often came here to escape from the world, just like you."

"Do you remember where he liked to go?" Lena asked.

Mrs. Grimsby thought for a moment. "He often sat in a little reading nook at the far end of the library. It was his favorite spot. Perhaps we should look there."

Lena followed the ghost through the library's winding aisles until they reached a small alcove with a cozy chair and a reading lamp. It was a quiet, hidden corner, perfect for getting lost in a book.

"This was his spot," Mrs. Grimsby said, her voice tinged with nostalgia. "He would spend hours here, reading in peace."

Lena began searching the area, checking under the chair, behind the cushions, and even inside the lamp's base. But there was no book to be found.

"It's not here," Lena said, feeling a little discouraged.

"Don't worry," Mrs. Grimsby reassured her. "We'll find it. There's another place we should check—the attic."

"The attic?" Lena asked, surprised.

"Yes," the ghost replied. "It's where we store books that are too damaged to be on the shelves. Perhaps the boy hid the book there, thinking it was a safe place."

Lena agreed, and together they made their way up the narrow staircase to the attic. The door creaked as Lena pushed it open, revealing a dusty, dimly lit space filled with old books, broken furniture, and cobwebs.

"It's a bit spooky up here," Lena admitted, trying to brush away a cobweb that had caught in her hair.

Mrs. Grimsby chuckled softly. "It's not so bad once you get used to it. Let's start looking."

They began searching through the piles of books, checking every dusty volume they could find. The attic was filled with forgotten treasures—old diaries, tattered storybooks, and even some handwritten manuscripts. But still, there was no sign of *The Lost Tale of Hollow Hill.*

Just as Lena was about to suggest they check another part of the library, she noticed a small wooden chest tucked away in a corner. It was locked, but the lock was old and rusty.

"Mrs. Grimsby, look!" Lena called, pointing to the chest. "Do you think it could be in there?"

Mrs. Grimsby floated over and examined the chest. "It's possible. This chest hasn't been opened in years. Let's see if we can unlock it."

Lena carefully pried at the rusty lock until it finally gave way with a loud snap. She opened the chest and gasped.

Inside was a small, leather-bound book with a faded title embossed on the cover: *The Lost Tale of Hollow Hill.*

"We found it!" Lena exclaimed, holding up the book.

Mrs. Grimsby's eyes filled with tears of joy. "Thank you, Lena. You've done what I couldn't do on my own. Now I can finally rest."

Lena smiled, feeling a warm glow of accomplishment. She handed the book to Mrs. Grimsby, who carefully placed it on a nearby shelf.

As the book touched the shelf, a soft, golden light surrounded Mrs. Grimsby. She turned to Lena with a peaceful smile.

"Thank you, dear," she said. "You've been a true friend. I'm so glad we met."

Before Lena could respond, Mrs. Grimsby began to fade, her form becoming more and more transparent until she disappeared completely, leaving only a faint shimmer in the air.

Lena stood in the attic, feeling both sad and happy at the same time. She knew she would miss Mrs. Grimsby, but she was glad that the ghost could finally find peace.

The next day, Lena returned to the library. She walked through the familiar aisles, her heart feeling a little lighter. She knew that Mrs. Grimsby was no longer there, but she could still feel the ghost's presence in the quiet corners of the library.

When she reached the Old Book Room, Lena noticed something different. The room seemed brighter, less dusty, and the air felt warmer. The books on the shelves seemed to glow with a soft light, as if they were happy to be there.

As Lena walked through the room, she spotted a new book lying on the table where she had first met Mrs. Grimsby. The title was *The Ghost in the Library: A Story of Friendship*.

Lena picked up the book and smiled. She knew that Mrs. Grimsby had left it for her, a reminder of their adventure and the special bond they had formed.

She sat down at the table and began to read, feeling a deep sense of contentment. She knew that, even though Mrs. Grimsby was gone, her spirit would always live on in the stories of the library.

And as long as there were readers like Lena, the library would never be a lonely place again.

The Candy Corn Curse

It was Halloween night, and four best friends—Jade, Leo, Mia, and Ethan—were out trick-or-treating in their neighborhood. The streets were filled with kids in costumes, laughing and running from house to house, collecting candy. The air was crisp, and the moon shone brightly in the sky, casting an eerie glow over everything.

The friends had decided to explore a part of the neighborhood they had never been to before. It was on the edge of town, where the houses were older and the streets were darker. They had heard rumors that strange things happened there on Halloween night, but they were too curious to stay away.

As they walked down the dimly lit street, they noticed an old, decrepit house at the end of the block. It was covered in ivy, with broken windows and a sagging roof. A single light flickered in one of the upstairs windows, giving the house a haunted appearance.

"Do you think anyone lives there?" Mia asked, her voice barely above a whisper.

"I don't know," Jade replied, staring at the house. "But it looks like something out of a horror movie."

"We should go check it out," Leo suggested, grinning mischievously.

"Are you crazy?" Ethan said, shaking his head. "That place looks seriously creepy."

But before they could decide what to do, the front door of the house creaked open, and an old woman stepped out onto the porch. She was hunched over, with wild gray hair and piercing blue eyes. She wore a tattered shawl around her shoulders and held a small bag in her hand.

The friends froze, unsure whether to run or stay.

The old woman's eyes locked onto them, and she slowly shuffled down the steps, stopping in front of them.

"Trick or treat," she said in a raspy voice, holding out the bag.

The friends exchanged uneasy glances. Something about the woman gave them the chills, but they didn't want to be rude.

"Uh, thank you," Jade said, hesitantly reaching out to take the bag.

The old woman's grip was surprisingly strong as she placed the bag in Jade's hand. "Beware the candy corn," she whispered, her eyes narrowing. "It carries a curse."

"A curse?" Leo repeated, raising an eyebrow.

The old woman nodded. "Ignore my warning, and you'll face the consequences. The candy corn will transform you, and you'll be trapped forever unless you work together to break the curse."

Without another word, the woman turned and shuffled back into the house, closing the door behind her with a loud creak.

The friends stood there in stunned silence, staring at the bag in Jade's hand.

"Do you think she was serious?" Mia asked, her voice trembling.

"It's probably just some weird Halloween prank," Ethan said,

"...I mean, candy can't be cursed, right?"

"Only one way to find out," Leo said with a smirk. He reached into the bag and pulled out a piece of candy corn. Before anyone could stop him, he popped it into his mouth.

"Leo, no!" Jade exclaimed, but it was too late.

Leo chewed and swallowed, then grinned at his friends. "See? Nothing to worry ab—"

But before he could finish his sentence, Leo's eyes widened, and he doubled over, clutching his stomach. The others watched in horror as his skin started to change color, turning a sickly green. His body began to grow and contort, his arms lengthening and his hands morphing into sharp claws. Within seconds, Leo had transformed into a scaly, green monster with glowing yellow eyes and sharp fangs.

"Leo!" Mia screamed, backing away in terror.

"What's happening to him?" Ethan yelled.

Leo tried to speak, but all that came out was a low, guttural growl. He looked down at his monstrous hands and let out a roar of despair.

"We have to help him!" Jade cried, frantically looking around. "The old woman said the candy was cursed! We need to break the curse!"

Before they could figure out what to do, Mia, who had been holding the bag of candy corn, accidentally dropped it. Several pieces scattered across the ground. In the chaos, Ethan and Jade each stepped on a piece, crushing them underfoot.

The moment they did, both of them began to change.

Ethan's skin turned pale as a ghost, his body becoming translucent. His legs vanished, leaving him floating a few inches above the ground. His eyes glowed an eerie blue, and he moaned as his voice became hollow and echoey. He had become a ghost.

Jade's transformation was different. Her hair turned bright orange, and her skin took on a pumpkin-like texture. Her hands became twisted vines, and her eyes glowed like jack-o'-lanterns. She was now part pumpkin, with a wicked grin carved into her face.

"Oh no, not me too!" Jade wailed, her voice distorted by her new pumpkin form.

Mia stood frozen in fear, clutching the last piece of candy corn in her hand. She looked at her friends, now transformed into Halloween creatures, and realized the gravity of the situation.

"What do we do?" Mia asked, her voice shaking. "How do we break the curse?"

Leo growled, Ethan moaned, and Jade's vine hands twitched helplessly. None of them knew the answer.

Mia knew they had to work together, just like the old woman had said. But how? What did she mean by "work together"?

Mia took a deep breath, trying to calm her racing heart. She looked at her transformed friends and knew she had to stay strong. They had to figure this out before the curse became permanent.

"Okay, let's think," Mia said, pacing back and forth. "The old woman said the candy corn was cursed and that we'd be trapped forever unless we worked together. There has to be a way to reverse this."

Leo, still in his monstrous form, growled softly and pointed to the bag of candy corn on the ground. Mia picked it up and noticed something strange. Inside the bag, along with the candy, was a small, folded piece of paper.

Mia unfolded the paper and read the message aloud:

To break the curse, you must face your fears and find the true spirit of Halloween. Only then will you be restored to your true selves.

"What does that even mean?" Jade asked, her jack-o'-lantern grin looking oddly cheerful despite the situation.

"I think it means we need to do something that scares us," Ethan said, his ghostly voice echoing. "Maybe if we confront our fears, the curse will be lifted."

"But what are we supposed to be afraid of?" Mia wondered. "And what's the 'true spirit of Halloween'?"

"I'm not sure," Ethan replied, his ghostly form shimmering, "but we have to try something before we're stuck like this forever."

Leo, still unable to speak, gestured toward the old woman's house. His glowing eyes conveyed a sense of urgency.

"You're right," Mia said, catching on. "Maybe we need to go back to where this all started. Let's go to the old woman's house and see if she can help us."

With Leo leading the way, the group cautiously approached the spooky old house. It loomed even more ominously in the moonlight, casting long, eerie shadows over the yard.

Mia knocked on the door, which creaked open on its own. The friends stepped inside, the floorboards groaning under their weight. The air was thick with the scent of dust and something else—something that smelled faintly of magic.

As they walked down the dark hallway, they noticed portraits on the walls. The faces in the paintings seemed to follow their every move, their eyes filled with sorrow and fear. The house was eerily silent, except for the faint ticking of a clock somewhere in the distance.

At the end of the hallway, they found a door slightly ajar. Pushing it open, they entered what appeared to be a study, filled with shelves of old books and strange, glowing artifacts.

And there, sitting in a high-backed chair by the fireplace, was the old woman.

"I see you've returned," she said, her voice as raspy as before. "Have you learned your lesson?"

Mia stepped forward, her heart pounding. "Please, we didn't mean to ignore your warning. We need to break the curse. How do we do it?"

The old woman's eyes glinted with a mix of kindness and mischief. "You must each face your deepest fear. Only then will the true spirit of Halloween reveal itself."

"What are our deepest fears?" Jade asked, feeling her vine-like hands curl in anxiety.

"That is for you to discover," the old woman replied. "But be warned, the clock is ticking. If you do not succeed by midnight, the curse will be permanent."

The friends exchanged worried glances. Midnight was only an hour away.

Determined to break the curse, the friends decided to split up and search the house for clues. They hoped that by confronting whatever scared them most, they would unlock the secret to reversing the curse.

Ethan floated down to the basement, where the darkness was thick and oppressive. He had always been afraid of the dark, and now, as a ghost, it seemed to press in on him from all sides. But he knew he had to be brave. As he floated deeper into the shadows, he heard a voice whispering his name. It was his own fear, trying to lure him into despair.

"No," Ethan said, standing his ground. "I'm not afraid of the dark anymore."

As soon as he spoke the words, the basement light flickered on, and he felt his ghostly form become more solid. He was still a ghost, but he had taken the first step toward breaking the curse.

Meanwhile, Jade found herself in the kitchen, where a massive pumpkin sat on the table, carved into a frightening face. She had always been scared of jack-o'-lanterns, ever since a particularly scary one had given her nightmares as a child. But now, as part pumpkin herself, she had to confront this fear.

She approached the jack-o'-lantern, feeling her heart race. "You don't scare me," she whispered, reaching out to touch it.

To her surprise, the jack-o'-lantern's face softened, and the light inside it dimmed to a warm glow. Jade's pumpkin skin began to feel less tight, and she knew she had passed her test.

Leo, still in his monstrous form, made his way to the attic. He had always been afraid of heights, and now, looking out of the attic's tiny window, he felt a surge of panic. The attic was high above the ground, and the only way to overcome his fear was to look out and face it.

With trembling hands, Leo forced himself to step closer to the window. He looked down at the world below, feeling dizzy, but he didn't turn away. "I'm not afraid of heights," he said firmly.

As he said the words, Leo felt his monstrous features soften slightly. He wasn't fully back to normal, but he had made progress.

Mia, holding the last piece of candy corn, stayed behind in the study with the old woman. Her greatest fear had always been letting her friends down, and now she felt the weight of their fate resting on her shoulders.

"I don't want to fail them," Mia said, tears welling up in her eyes.

The old woman looked at her kindly. "You haven't failed them, dear. You've been their leader, their strength. Now, you just need to believe in yourself."

Mia closed her eyes and took a deep breath. "I'm not afraid of failing," she whispered.

As soon as she said the words, the last piece of candy corn dissolved in her hand, and a warm light filled the room.

The friends regrouped in the study, each of them feeling a little more like themselves. The old woman watched them with a proud smile.

"You have faced your fears," she said. "Now, the true spirit of Halloween can be revealed."

Suddenly, the room was filled with a warm, golden light. The friends felt their bodies shift and change, their monstrous forms melting away as they returned to their true selves.

As the light faded, they looked at each other in relief. They were back to normal!

"You did it!" Mia exclaimed, hugging her friends.

The old woman stood and approached them. "The true spirit of Halloween isn't about fear or curses. It's about bravery, friendship, and the courage to face what scares you most. Remember that, and you will always find your way."

The friends thanked the old woman and left the house, feeling lighter and happier than they had all night. The clock struck midnight as they stepped back onto the street, and they knew the curse was broken for good.

As they walked home, they passed out candy to the few remaining trick-or-treaters, grateful for the adventure they had shared.

And from that Halloween on, they knew that no matter what spooky challenges came their way, they could face them together.

The Ghostly Game of Tag

It was a chilly afternoon on Halloween when a group of friends—Emma, Ben, Lily, and Max—decided to play a game of tag in the neighborhood park. The trees were nearly bare, their branches reaching up like skeletal fingers toward the overcast sky. The air was filled with the scent of fallen leaves and the excitement of Halloween night just hours away.

The friends ran through the park, laughing and dodging each other as they played. Emma was "It," and she was determined to catch Ben, who was the fastest runner among them. Just as she was about to tag him, a thick, eerie fog rolled in, covering the park in a dense blanket of white.

"Where did this fog come from?" Lily asked, her voice tinged with concern as the fog grew thicker, making it hard to see.

"I don't know," Max replied, squinting to see through the mist. "But it's getting really hard to see. Maybe we should head back."

"Yeah, let's go," Ben agreed. "This is kind of creepy."

But as they turned to leave, they realized that the park looked completely different. The familiar playground was gone, replaced by an old, dilapidated one that looked like it hadn't been used in years. The swings creaked eerily, and the merry-go-round was covered in rust.

"This isn't the park," Emma said, her voice trembling. "Where are we?"

Before anyone could answer, they heard the sound of children's laughter echoing through the fog. But the laughter wasn't coming from them—it was coming from somewhere else, somewhere close.

"Who's there?" Max called out, trying to sound brave.

The laughter stopped abruptly, replaced by an eerie silence. Then, out of the fog, figures began to appear—children, dressed in old-fashioned clothes, their faces pale and slightly transparent.

"Ghosts!" Lily gasped, stepping back in fear.

The ghostly children floated closer, their expressions mischievous.

"Want to play a game?" one of the ghosts asked, grinning wickedly.

The friends exchanged nervous glances. They had no idea how they had ended up here, but it was clear that these ghosts wanted something from them.

"What kind of game?" Ben asked cautiously.

"Tag," the ghost replied. "Just like you were playing before. But here's the twist—if you get tagged, you become one of us. And if all of you get tagged before the game is over, you'll be stuck here in our playground forever."

Emma's heart pounded in her chest. This was no ordinary game of tag—it was a game with their very lives at stake.

"But if we win?" Max asked, trying to keep his voice steady.

"If you win," the ghost said, "you get to go back to your world. The rules are simple: don't get tagged, and stay in the boundaries of the playground. Ready or not, here we come!"

Before the friends could protest, the ghosts scattered, their eerie laughter filling the air. The game had begun.

The friends wasted no time. They ran in different directions, trying to put as much distance between themselves and the ghosts as possible. But the playground was small, and the fog made it difficult to see where they were going.

Emma darted behind a large slide, her heart racing. She could hear the faint footsteps of the ghosts as they moved through the playground, searching for their next victim.

Ben, the fastest of the group, climbed up the jungle gym, hoping to get a better view of the area. From his vantage point, he could see the entire playground, but the fog made it hard to spot the others. He knew he had to stay alert—one wrong move, and he could get tagged.

Lily and Max stuck together, hiding behind an old, rusted merry-go-round. They were both scared, but they knew they had to stay calm if they were going to make it out of this ghostly playground.

"We have to think of a plan," Max whispered to Lily. "We can't just keep running forever."

Lily nodded, her eyes darting around as she tried to come up with an idea. "Maybe if we can find the boundaries of the playground, we can figure out a way to escape."

"But we can't leave the boundaries," Max reminded her. "The ghosts said we have to stay within them."

Lily frowned, realizing he was right. "Then we need to find a way to trick the ghosts. If we can get them to chase us into a trap, maybe we can tag them instead."

Max thought about it for a moment. "That could work, but we'd have to be really careful. If we get tagged, it's game over."

Meanwhile, Emma was trying to stay hidden behind the slide when she heard the sound of footsteps approaching. She held her breath, hoping the ghost wouldn't find her. But as the footsteps grew closer, she knew she couldn't stay hidden forever.

Thinking quickly, Emma crawled out from behind the slide and dashed toward the swings. She could hear the ghost right behind her, but she didn't look back. She just kept running, hoping to find somewhere else to hide.

Ben watched from the top of the jungle gym as Emma ran, the ghost hot on her heels. He knew he had to do something to help her.

"Over here!" Ben shouted, waving his arms to get the ghost's attention.

The ghost turned its head toward Ben, giving Emma a few precious seconds to escape. She quickly changed direction, running toward the old seesaw on the other side of the playground.

The ghost floated up to the jungle gym, its eyes locked on Ben. "You're next," it hissed.

Ben's heart pounded as he quickly climbed down the jungle gym and sprinted away, the ghost following close behind.

Back at the merry-go-round, Lily and Max had come up with a plan. They decided to use the merry-go-round as a decoy. If they could get one of the ghosts to chase them around it, they could trap the ghost by spinning the merry-go-round fast enough to confuse it.

"Ready?" Max whispered.

"Ready," Lily replied, her heart pounding in her chest.

Max took a deep breath and stepped out from behind the merry-go-round. He waved his arms, trying to get the attention of one of the ghosts. "Hey, over here!"

One of the ghosts, a young boy with a mischievous grin, spotted Max and floated toward him. Max turned and ran, leading the ghost around the merry-go-round.

Lily waited until the ghost was close, then she pushed the merry-go-round with all her might, causing it to spin rapidly. The ghost, caught off guard, tried to follow Max, but the spinning merry-go-round made it dizzy and confused.

Taking advantage of the ghost's disorientation, Max and Lily quickly ducked under the merry-go-round and escaped to the other side.

"It worked!" Lily whispered excitedly.

"But we have to do more," Max said. "We need to find the others and see if we can trick the other ghosts too."

Meanwhile, Ben and Emma had managed to regroup near the old slide. They knew they couldn't keep running forever, so they decided to come up with their own plan.

"We need to lure them into one place," Ben said. "If we can get all the ghosts together, we might be able to trick them like Lily and Max did."

"But how do we get them all in one place?" Emma asked.

Ben thought for a moment. "What if we pretend to get caught? If the ghosts think they've won, they'll all come together to tag us. Then we can make our move."

Emma hesitated, knowing it was a risky plan, but she nodded. "Okay, let's do it."

The two of them ran toward the center of the playground, calling out to the ghosts. "We give up!" Ben shouted. "You win!"

The ghosts, hearing Ben's voice, quickly converged on the center of the playground. They circled around Ben and Emma, their grins widening as they prepared to tag them.

But just as the ghosts reached out to tag them, Ben and Emma ducked and rolled out of the way, causing the ghosts to collide with each other. The ghosts, confused and disoriented, began to argue among themselves.

"Now!" Ben shouted.

Emma and Ben sprinted toward the merry-go-round, where Lily and Max were waiting. Together, they quickly pushed the merry-go-round, causing it to spin faster and faster.

The ghosts, still disoriented from their collision, tried to chase after the friends, but the spinning merry-go-round made it impossible for them to focus.

As the merry-go-round spun, the friends noticed that the fog around the playground began to lift, revealing a path that led out of the ghostly playground.

"Look!" Lily shouted, pointing to the path. "That must be the way out!"

The friends didn't waste any time. They ran toward the path, leaving the confused ghosts behind. As they reached the edge of the playground, they could see the familiar sight of their neighborhood park in the distance.

"We did it!" Max exclaimed, his heart pounding with relief.

The friends sprinted down the path, the fog dissipating behind them. As they crossed the boundary back into their own world, they felt a wave of warmth and light wash over them.

They stopped to catch their breath, looking back at the park. The ghostly playground had disappeared, replaced by the familiar playground they knew and loved. The sun was setting, casting a warm orange glow over everything.

"We're back!" Emma said, smiling with relief.

"Just in time for Halloween," Ben added, looking at the Halloween decorations that now lined the streets.

The friends hugged each other, grateful to be back in their own world.

They had faced their fears, outsmarted the ghosts, and returned to their Halloween night adventure.

As they walked home, they couldn't help but laugh about their spooky adventure. They knew that this Halloween would be one they'd never forget.

And as they passed out candy to trick-or-treaters and enjoyed the night, they couldn't help but smile, knowing they had survived the ghostly game of tag.

Made in United States
Orlando, FL
26 October 2024

53107502R00086